The Vision Board

TangoBird

The Purpose of the Vision Board

The purpose of the vision board is to curate the future of your dreams. Use these photos and affirmations to piece together the life you were destined to have.

How to Create a Vision Board

Get clear on what it is you'd like to call in at this time & collect photos that represent & align with the vision of the future you would like to attract. As you create this visual, really feel yourself a part of it.

This will help bridge the gap between your current self & future self and help attract the new reality effortlessly by giving you the sensation of it already being real.

Scan below for exclusive access, content, bonuses, huge promotions, surprises & more...

Scan Code

EVERYTHING
ALWAYS
WORKS OUT
FOR ME

MIRACLES
happen
TO ME
every single day

I always get
princess treatment.

I invite in an abundance of love from all directions.

Unconditional love is my birthright.

Purpose fuels passion.

Enjoy life to the fullest.

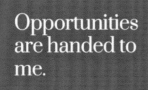

Opportunities are handed to me.

Traveling all the time is my reality

I live in a state of
perpetual happiness

I RELEASE ANY
blockages
HOLDING ME BACK
from recieving love

I live a life of Rest
and Relaxation

REPOSE

THE MORE
I love myself,
THE MORE
love surrounds me

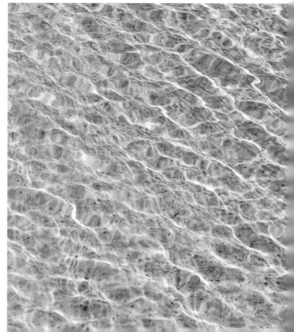

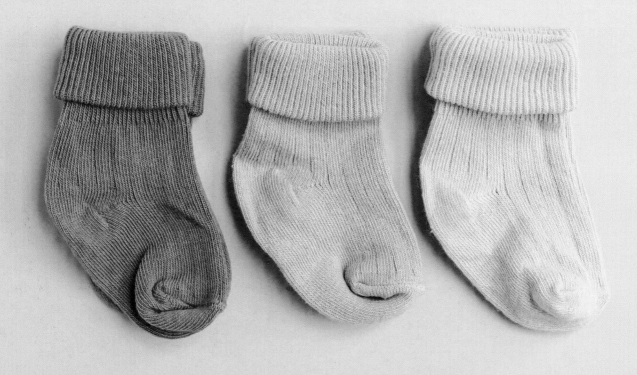

I am in
alignment with
unconditional
love.

IT IS A
privilege
TO BE IN MY
presence

I receive just by
existing.

EVERY PENNY
I spend,
IS RETUNRED
to me tenfold.

ery day, my

and blessings

multiply.

MY PRESENCE IS A PRIVILEGE.

MY PRESENCE IS A PRIVILEGE.

My mind is worth millions.

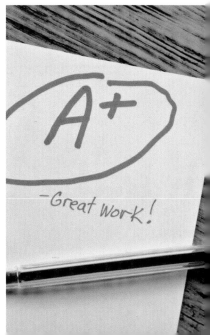

MY EXISTENCE PAYS FOR ITSELF.

I invite
immense
luck into
my life

BRICK LANE E.I.
ব্রিক লেন

I AM ENOUGH,
just as I am,
DESERVING OF
love and respect

I deserve
good things

I DON'T WORK
for money,
MONEY WORKS
for me

Reminder

Everything I desire, desires me more.

Okay!

How am I so
lucky?

Reminder

The Universe takes chances
on me.

Okay!

Opportunities
find me
everywhere I go.

I EXPERIENCE
once in a lifetime
OPPORTUNITIES
multiple times a day

I am now
stepping into the
identity of my
next level.

Universe, show me
how it gets better.

It is always
working out for
me.

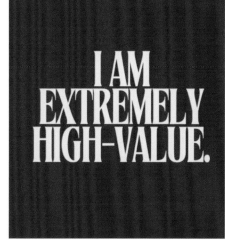

I AM
EXTREMELY
HIGH-VALUE.

It is a privilege
to be in my
presence.

I AM IN CONTROL

I am in alignment with the frequency of generational wealth

Next 92 km

Congrats! You've been verified.

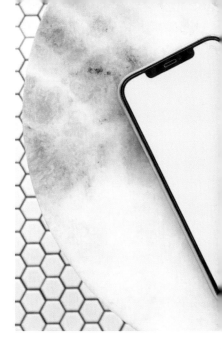

I attract
opportunities
effortlessly

GO GREEN

MY CIRCLES
EMPOWER
ME

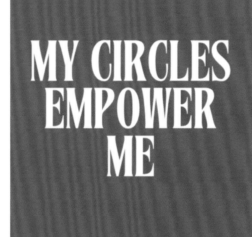

I am a money

magnet

I am
so
lucky

IT IS SAFE FOR ME TO BE LOVED.

LOVE
finds me
EVERYWHERE,
effortlessly

The more wealth in
my hands, the more
good circulates in
the Universe.

My energy is expensive & addicting

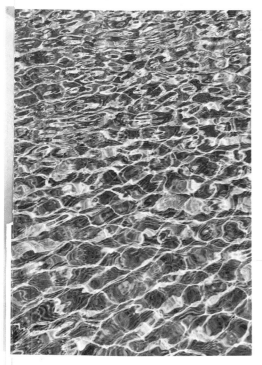